Serving in the Kitchen

Serving in the Kitchen

Serving in the Kitchen

Books by Mrs. White

For the Love of Christian Homemaking

Mother's Book of Home Economics

Living on His Income

Economy for the Christian Home

Mother's Hour

At Mother's House

Introduction to Home Economics

Early Morning Revival Challenge

Prentiss Study Deluxe Edition

Mother's Faith

Old Fashioned Motherhood

An Old Fashioned Budget

Homemaking for Happiness

Gracious House Keeping

(Cover photograph by Mrs. Sharon White: Flowers on the Table at our Home in Vermont.)

Serving in the Kitchen

Cookbook with Recipes, Advice, and Encouragement

For the Christian Home

By Mrs. Sharon White

All rights reserved. No portion of this book may be copied without permission from the publisher.

All Scripture Quotations are from the King James Bible.

Copyright 2023 by Mrs. Sharon White and The Legacy of Home Press:

All photographs are from Mrs. White's home and are protected under copyright law.

ISBN Number: 978-1-956616-19-4

Serving in the Kitchen: Cookbook with Recipes, Advice, and Encouragement for the Christian Home

Author: Mrs. Sharon White

The Legacy of Home Press

Vermont - U.S.A.

Contents

Introduction ... 9

Part 1

Kitchen Help ... 11

A Selection of Tips and Ideas

Homemade Pantry	13
Spreading a Bountiful Table	15
Portions	16
Keeping a Full Pantry	18
Scheduled Meals	19
Teaching Children to Help	24
How to Acquire Pretty Things for the Kitchen	27
Picnics and Journeys	27
Packing Children's Lunches	29
Taking Care of the Sick and Injured	30
Food Budget	30
Holiday Dinners	32

Setting up Family Recipes — 33

Called to the Table — 35

The Dinner Hour — 36

Part 2

Serving Meals and House Specials — 39

Breakfast — 41

Lunch — 49

Dinner — 59

Part 3

Recipes — 67

Hamburger / Vegetable Soup over Mashed Potatoes — 71

Whole Wheat Molasses Bread — 75

Cheese Lasagna — 81

Beef Stew — 85

Whole Wheat Biscuits — 89

Simple Vegetable Soup — 93

Fettuccini Alfredo with Broccoli — 97

Challah Bread   101

Refrigerator Baked Potatoes   107

Homemade Frozen Pizzas   111

Italian Bread   117

Chocolate Chip Oat Muffins   123

Cinnamon Applesauce Cake   127

Oatmeal Chocolate Chip Cookies   131

Olive Oil Cookies   135

Mini Chocolate Chip Cookies   139

General Index   145

About the Author   147

~ I have a miniature book I keep on the hutch in our parlour. It is called, "Give us This Day: The Lord's Prayer." It was illustrated by Tasha Tudor and published in 1987. You can see this little book in the photograph on page 132. ~

Serving in the Kitchen

"But my God shall supply all your need according to his riches in glory by Christ Jesus." – Philippians 4:19

Introduction

As a young girl in school, starting at the age of 12, I took a three year course of home economics. The school employed two teachers with two large classrooms. Students were assigned their own kitchen and a dining room table. There were 4 or 5 kitchens, set up in stalls, along the back wall of each room. There were at least 2 girls for each kitchen and we worked together as we learned all about homemaking.

The curriculum included lessons in child care and family relationships, sewing, cooking, baking, and nutrition. We were taught how to wash dishes and keep a sanitary kitchen. We learned how to set the table and how to prepare food for a family.

I remember seeing some of the boys walking down the hall. They were drawn to the open doorway of the classroom. They could smell the food cooking and they would ask, with a wistful look, "What are you making today?" It would be bread or pizza. It gave them a yearning for home.

This feeling for home is what draws many to a kitchen when good food is being prepared. I have noticed that when a stew has been simmering on the stove for hours, there is a welcoming scent in the air. But when we heat up a frozen dinner in the microwave, or warm up something out of a can, something is missing.

There is love and genuine hard work in preparing home-cooked meals. It is an act of much needed service.

Serving in the Kitchen

Modern teaching says we need to make life easy and find shortcuts in the kitchen. It is common to pay others to prepare our food and to do those acts of service that used to be done at home by mothers and grandmothers. Any meaningful work is not going to be easy. But there is going to be a reward when we do the traditional work ourselves. We will be creating memories, saving money, and making life pretty and restful for our guests and family. Homemaking and cooking are always going to be worth the effort.

Many are looking for a simpler, old fashioned life. What used to be considered ordinary is what we now crave. We want rest and peace and a pleasant home. One of the most important aspects of homemaking is maintaining an economical kitchen and feeding the family with wholesome, nourishing food. This does not cost very much and can bring great rewards. Even a humble home, with a family of limited means, is considered rich if they have a supply of quality food.

In this book you will find three sections to help inspire you to labor in the kitchen. The first part is full of a variety of tips and ideas from my own experience. They are listed under subject headings for easy reference. The second part offers brief serving suggestions and menu ideas for breakfast, lunch, and dinner. The final section contains a sampling of 16 recipes from my kitchen. There are photographs for each recipe along with detailed instructions.

Sprinkled throughout the book will be Bible verses, hymns, pictures from my home, and prayers. I hope this gives you a sense of visiting me in my own kitchen. May you be blessed in your efforts of building up the home with cheer and love.

Serving in the Kitchen

~ *Part 1* ~
Kitchen Help

Serving in the Kitchen

~ *For a Joyful Heart* ~

"And be ye kind one to another, tenderhearted, forgiving one another, even as God for Christ's sake hath forgiven you."

Ephesians 4:32

"Speaking to yourselves in psalms and hymns and spiritual songs, singing and making melody in your heart to the Lord; Giving thanks always for all things unto God and the Father in the name of our Lord Jesus Christ."

Ephesians 5:19 - 20

{Photograph on previous page: "Flowers on the table at our Home."}

~ Kitchen Help ~

A Selection of Tips and Ideas

Homemade Pantry

This week I made cinnamon cake, cookies, muffins, and biscuits. When that supply begins to get low, I will make more. When we make a lot of our own food from scratch we are providing the family with a homemade pantry.

Try to have a supply of freshly baked cookies, muffins, or quick bread. These are more filling than store bought treats and will make the rest of the food last longer.

A well stocked kitchen should be full of ingredients so we can make anything we need at any time. There is no need to go to the store for missing items. There is no need to go out to eat at a restaurant. Going out on errands for shopping and such will wear us out. It is tiring work. When we are able to stay home more, we are more peaceful and rested. There will be no need to go out on constant errands when we have everything we need at home.

Serving in the Kitchen

Here is an old time example from literature in 1908:

Grace Livingston Hill wrote about a homemade pantry in her book, "Marcia Schuyler." In the main character's new home, she found freshly made bread and other homemade food that was expected to last for days. This would give her time to make more bread, pies, and cakes after she got settled. When she first looked around her new kitchen, to see what food was available, she found it amply supplied by her new aunts:

"There was a leg of lamb beautifully cooked, half a dozen pies, their flaky crusts bearing witness to the culinary skill of the aunts, a fruit cake, a pound cake, a jar of delectable cookies, and another of fat sugary doughnuts, three loaves of bread, and a sheet of puffy rusks with their shining tops dusted with sugar. Besides, the preserve closet was rich in all kinds of preserves, jellies, and pickles."

("Marcia Schuyler," by GLH, page 101.)

When we put in the effort to prepare food in advance, we save money and time. An empty, cold kitchen can tempt a tired, hungry soul to constantly run to the store. Remember this bit of advice: *Make things before you need them.* This is an essential quality in being a capable and efficient housekeeper.

Spreading a Bountiful Table

Many of us cannot afford to buy expensive food like lobster, steak, and gourmet dishes. It is not really a frugal way to live. Most people don't really like to eat like that anyway. They prefer home cooking and traditional dishes.

It doesn't cost a lot of money to provide a nice display of food. The key is to serve a variety of carefully portioned food and to set an inviting table.

When we put out napkins, silverware, and a few dishes at each place, it makes the experience of dining more pleasant.

It is common for the table to be set with fresh bread and butter, vegetables or a garden salad, the main course, side dishes, and a nice beverage of milk, coffee, tea, or ice water. It will look like a feast is being served.

There are days in the summer when my grown children will come home, with my grandchildren, and bring food. They may have been out on errands and stopped on their way home. I would be given a bag of groceries with things like beverages, ingredients for a good lunch, and some dessert. I would gratefully prepare a good meal that would feed all of us.

Sometimes when we are expecting company, we are tempted to go out and buy a bunch of food that we don't normally have. This is wonderful if you can afford it, and perhaps it may be possible for special occasions. But a carefully set table of nicely made food, with a cheerful hostess, will bring just as much happiness to your guests.

Portions

Too much sugar in the diet will cause you to eat more than necessary. The more sugar you eat, the more hungry you will feel. Instead, eat more whole grains, fresh fruit, and vegetables. These are more nourishing and filling.

To avoid waste, give children a small amount of food and drink at a time. They can always have seconds and thirds if they like, but always serve these in small portions.

Try to notice the different likes and dislikes of the family. When we serve a variety of things at the table, including an assortment of vegetables and fresh bread, everyone will have the opportunity to find a few of their favorites. A good way to teach the children about service and kindness is to politely ask if they would like sauce on their pasta. Or, would they like a serving of corn? Do they want butter on their bread? These questions are an example of being a good hostess. The children will appreciate it very much.

I don't like the idea of forcing little ones to eat. There should be no battle or sadness at the dinner table. Let it be a place of rest and refreshment. We want children to grow up loving home and loving the memories of delicious home cooking.

If you have eaten a normal portion at mealtime and still feel hungry. Try getting up and doing some activity or take a walk around the house. Then keep busy and wait for the next mealtime to eat again.

My mother used to cook just enough food for our meals. This avoided waste. She had learned, through practice, exactly how much she needed to give each of us. Sometimes she would reserve a little of the meat for sandwiches to go in Dad's lunch for work the following day.

A certain portion for each meal will give us comfort and a sense of contentment. It reminds me of the Lord's Prayer, when we ask: *"Give us this day, our daily bread."*

Keeping a Full Pantry

Try not to let the pantry supplies get low. I don't want my husband or children to panic or worry because we are running out of food. A refrigerator and freezer that are empty is a sad state. When that happens we may feel poor and desperate. Hard times come to all of us in certain seasons and these moments are not pleasant. But the goal is to always do our best to keep our kitchen well stocked with quality food.

I have a bookcase in our guest room. I try to keep this full of things like crackers, canned vegetables, extra baking supplies, boxes of pasta, canisters of oatmeal, and coffee and tea. We also have some cabinets and shelves in the kitchen for more food storage.

Sometimes we use up far more than necessary. This might be the case with such things as ketchup or ranch dressing. It is important to get by and make do until the next shopping trip. Beware of constantly replacing expensive ingredients that are non-essentials.

In our rural mountain village in northern Vermont, we have bitterly cold winters. We must keep a full pantry because it is an ordeal to travel in such weather. Our winters are long and cold. We need to have plenty of food much like we need a large supply of wood for our heat. Living here for more than 20 years has taught me how important it is to be prepared.

I keep about 20 pounds of flour in my refrigerator at all times. I use this almost daily for muffins, cookies, cakes, and bread. I keep a couple of tins of baking powder, baking soda, and a jar of yeast. I have a few bags of brown sugar and packages of margarine in a drawer in the refrigerator. This is where I also keep a large bag of chocolate chips I portion out for cookies and muffins. This supply will last me a long time. As I go along, I replace what I use when I am able to get to a store.

My mother-in-law would make a great deal of food and then neatly package and store it all in the refrigerator. When we would go over for a visit she would say, "There are baked potatoes all ready to heat up. There is fresh salad in there. I just made meatballs for sandwiches and there is some spaghetti in that bag on the top shelf." She had enough food for her family and guests, all prepared, to last for days. We would just warm up what we wanted and then all sit down together at the table.

Scheduled Meals

A routine brings order and security. It is always good to know when we are going to eat. This is a comfort to children. The meals should be scheduled at the same time each day.

I would not ask the children what they wanted for dinner. This can lead to a habit of being ill-prepared. It can be annoying when Mom is always saying to the family, "What do you want for dinner?" If there is already a plan in place to serve regular, simple meals, there is less stress and less annoyance. There is also a bit of fun and mystery when Mom is happily cooking in the kitchen. Husband and children may wonder what she is making. When they are called to the table, they will be happy and delighted, eager to enjoy a good meal.

In my childhood home we had assigned seating at the dinner table. I also did this with my own children and now my grandchildren. It keeps things orderly and peaceful.

Set the table in a nice and inviting way. This sets the stage for a happy time. There are far too many distractions and temptations to keep us busy and occupied at all hours of the day and night. When we do our best to set a beautiful table, serving wholesome food in a more formal way, we bring culture, refinement, and elegance into the humblest of homes. This helps cheer the hearts and provides a bright spot in their day. This brings a welcomed and expected rest from the weariness of life and the troubles around us.

When we go to some effort to make the table look lovely, people are not as likely to eat and run off. Wouldn't that make the hostess feel bad? We cultivate good manners when we sit together and take the time to eat a leisurely meal with thanksgiving and gratefulness.

When someone will not be home for dinner, it is common to reserve a plate of food to give them when they return.

Years ago, one of my sons (a young adult at the time) had an evening shift at work. After dinner, I would fill a plate for him and then wrap it up and put it on a shelf in the refrigerator. I would write a note and leave it on the table before I went to sleep. In the morning, I would find a note of thanks from him. Here are a few samples from those letters, which I have saved in a remembrance folder:

Mom's note: (Sample one)

Supper is on the blue plate, 2nd shelf.
Beef Stroganoff and Carrots.
Have a piece of Blueberry / Lemon Cake on counter.
Love Mom

His response: Thanks Mom, it was delicious!

Serving in the Kitchen

> Mom's note: (Sample two)
>
> Dinner is on the 2nd shelf, blue plate.
> BBQ Meatloaf, Mashed Potatoes, Green Beans.
> Bag of 2 pieces of bread with butter, garlic and parmesan.
> Love Mom
>
> His response: Thank you Mom! It was amazing!

> Mom's note: (Sample three)
>
> Dinner is in the small casserole pan.
> A quick Shepherd's Pie.
>
> His response: Thanks Mom!

During this time, my husband was also working a late shift so I was putting aside two dinners each night. Here are more samples from the notes:

> Mom's note: (Sample four)
>
> Top shelf, large circle pizza on the left is yours.
> (The other one is Dad's.)
> 450 degrees for 13 – 16 minutes.
> Love Mom.
>
> His response: Thanks Mom, Love you!

Serving in the Kitchen

> Mom's note: (Sample five)
>
> There are two blue dinner plates.
> One is Dad's.
> One is yours.
> They are both the same: Chicken, stuffing, corn, and potatoes.
> Love Mom
>
> ---
>
> His response: Thanks Mom! It was really good!

My husband and son appreciated that they did not have to miss out on a homemade dinner. They both looked forward to coming home and seeing that a special plate was reserved just for them.

A few years later my son was working as a chef, managing a kitchen in an upscale restaurant. One night after work he brought home a special treat for me. The following morning, I found a note on the counter. I still have it, all these years later. It said, "Chocolate Mousse in fridge on dessert plate is for *MOM*." He signed it with love.

Teaching Children to Help

When Mother is cheerful and has a good attitude about housework, children are eager to help.

Remind the children of this important rule: We must wash our hands before we enter the kitchen. Girls must put their hair up before they begin to work.

A child as young as 9 years old may be ready to start learning to cook and bake, depending on their level of responsibility and maturity. It is good to start with making toast and waffles. They can make sandwiches and serve cereal. Eventually, they will be ready to learn how to make scrambled eggs and homemade muffins. An adult should be monitoring them at all times to maintain safety. Mom should be the one to put the pans in and out of the oven.

Younger children can wash the highchair and table. They can tuck in chairs and do the sweeping. I have a child sized broom in our kitchen, along with a full size one. This makes it easier for the little ones to work when they have tools in their own size.

Serving in the Kitchen

Children can also wash dishes. They can learn to carefully dry them and put them away.

A Recipe for Washing Dishes

Begin cleaning and washing dishes immediately after each meal and snack. Everything is easier to clean when you do it right away.

Start with a clean, empty sink.

Start filling the sink with hot, soapy water.

Put in silverware and cups. Start washing these right away and placing them in the dish drainer.

When the cups and silverware are finished, fill the sink with bowls and plates.

Dry all the cups and silverware and put them away. This will leave plenty of room for the next batch of dishes to dry.

Next, wash the bowls and plates. Put them in the dish drainer. Dry them and put them away.

Now wash any pots and pans, putting them in the dish drainer as you go along. Dry and put them away.

Drain the sink, wipe it down, and enjoy a clean kitchen.

Serving in the Kitchen

This is a good time to teach children how to serve others with care and kindness. When some of my grandchildren are here for breakfast, I call one of them over to help me serve. I put 4 homemade muffins on a plate and hand it to the little hostess. She walks around to each person, each "guest," at the table and says, "Would you like one?" The guest is instructed to say either "Yes, please." Or, "No, thank you." The guest is then allowed to choose one of the muffins, taking it politely and putting it on his own plate. The children always smile while this ceremony is going on. One day the hostess said to me, after doing this duty, "Why don't we just pass out the muffins? It would be quicker." I smiled and said, "How else will everyone learn their manners?"

When my own children were young, they all had assigned work in the kitchen. One was the breakfast hostess, one was the lunch hostess, and one was in charge of the dinner hour. They prepared a simple meal and graciously served the family. I have a photograph of them, from many years ago, with some of the children sitting happily in their place. Two of the older girls (probably around 9 and 10 years old) capably served the food to the younger ones. They all looked so precious!

When children begin helping with the chores at a young age, it becomes a natural habit for them. They are learning life skills that will benefit them all of their lives.

How to Acquire Pretty Things for the Kitchen

Would you like a dinner bell, a pretty teapot, some tablecloths, and a nice set of dishes? How about a beautiful new pattern of silverware? In the past, these things may have been collected in a hope chest or set up in a wedding registry. If we don't already have nice things for the home, it might be a good idea to save up and buy a few things at a time. This can be done on special occasions such as an anniversary or birthday. Over time, perhaps a few years, you will have some lovely things to help cheer and brighten the dinner table.

Picnics and Journeys

I have a "picnic purse" which is really a pretty insulated lunch bag. I keep crackers in there and other little snacks. Whenever I leave the house, even just for a quick errand, this purse always goes with me. It saves a great deal of money when on outings because I always have my own food.

We have to take frequent trips to a hospital in the next state for medical care. The journey is too far for a day trip so we have to spend the night in a hotel. We always bring along our own food in a cooler or insulated bag. Hotels have microwaves and refrigerators which makes it easy to store and heat up food. We

Serving in the Kitchen

bring little bowls (with lids) full of homemade soup, pasta or cheese ravioli, salad, rolls, fruit, homemade muffins, and cookies or brownies. I also keep a supply of plastic silverware, napkins, and paper plates in our bag. This saves us both money and time so we can just rest at the hotel after the long drive.

The dining experience in a hotel room does not feel very home-like. I always bring a foldable bed tray with me. I use a cloth napkin on the tray, much as one would put a tablecloth on a table. The tray makes breakfasting and lunching away from home much more restful and enjoyable.

For a traditional picnic, bring a blanket to spread out on the ground. (This can later be kept in a zippered storage bag and used just for such outings.) Use a large thermos for the beverage and bring little cups to go around. Pack sandwiches, fruit, and cookies, along with napkins, in an insulated cooler. You can pack this kind of picnic anytime you have to be away from home during mealtime.

There used to be a water fountain at nearly every place we would go. Even the supermarkets had public fountains for their customers. Since the sale of water bottles has become so popular, the fountains are not as common. When I was growing up, I don't think they sold water in little bottles. It was free in most public places. In the days of "Little House on the Prairie," the family would travel near natural sources of water. They would stop and rest beside a cold spring and fill a container for the rest of their trip. A good option for today would be to bring your own ice water on your travels. You could use a stainless steel travel mug or a glass mason jar with a lid. Water is much better for us than an expensive bottle of soda or juice when we are away from home.

Packing Children's Lunches

In previous generations, a packed lunch included a sandwich, fruit, and home-baked cookies. Sometimes a child would get a piece of mom's apple pie or cake to go with their sandwich. It was a simple but filling lunch.

These days there is an incredible variety of snack-sized food available to go into a child's lunch bag for school. It is exciting and tempting to look at all the different treats in the store. But these are also very expensive. The main problem with these types of snacks is that they may contain a lot of sugar and are processed to the point that the child is still hungry and not getting enough nourishment. This type of food also makes children irritable and unhappy without realizing the cause of their difficult behavior. It is very sad! If you enjoy these treats, consider offering them sparingly while including fresh vegetables, fruit, and whole grains as their main food.

Taking Care of the Sick and Injured

It is important to keep a supply of special food, medicine, first aid supplies, and ice packs in case someone is suddenly taken ill. We have to adjust the diet of the sick patient by offering such things as: broth, jello, saltine crackers, and ginger ale. If you already have these things in your pantry for just such an emergency, there is no need to panic or run to the store. You will be able to calmly tend to the patient, keeping them comfortable, and helping them to get well.

It would be useful to keep a bed tray in the house. When I was home sick from school, as a child, my mother would bring me homemade chicken soup on a bed tray. It was comforting and helpful to be able to rest in bed without having to get up to eat at the kitchen table.

Food Budget

The household account is often managed by the wife and mother of the family. This money is mostly expected to pay for food and general grocery items. It is essential that we spend less than the budgeted amount while still providing the home with all that is needed.

A common way of doing this is to make a shopping list after looking through the kitchen to see what we are running low on. When we usually make the same type of food, it is simple to see what we actually need. Most lists include things like bread, butter, milk, eggs, and baking supplies.

Watch the store flyers to see the lowest prices on things you need. Plan your meals around what is available at a good price. Be willing to adjust the menu when necessary. For example, if you wanted to make hamburgers but the price is higher than normal, see if chicken is on sale instead. This is a wise and frugal use of money. It is not a good idea to pay high prices for things you know will go down in price in a week or two. It is important to learn to buy what we can afford and live within our means. Our meals do not have to be fancy or expensive.

Pay attention to what is already in the house. Gather what is ready from the garden. Avoid wasting food by eating what is available. For instance, if I have apples at home, I would have to eat them before they spoil. Having an apple for a snack would be a choice I made instead of eating something else, like cookies, cheese, or yogurt. We shouldn't be eating based on our mood or what we feel like having. We eat what is nutritious, what is on hand, and what we can afford. When you get into the habit of being economical you become a valued and capable asset to the household. But to bring cheer and happiness to one's heart, serve the apple baked in muffins, cake, or on a pretty plate with cinnamon.

Consider having a garden. When there is fresh lettuce, cucumbers, and peas available, this provides a portion of the day's food. Home grown produce will save a lot of money on groceries. On our property, we have strawberry plants and blueberry bushes which come back year after year. It doesn't bring a large crop but it is enough so that I rarely have to buy them in the store.

Spend carefully from a modest purse by choosing plain, wholesome ingredients and then make quality food at home.

Holiday Dinners

Inviting the family over for Thanksgiving or Christmas dinner is a wonderful event. It is good to have an extra table (or card table) which can be folded and stored away when not in use. This is very helpful to provide extra seating for a crowd.

Sometimes it is good to write out place-cards so the seating is already planned in advance. Both children and adults enjoy looking at the notes to see where they are supposed to sit.

This is the time to get out the best serving pieces and dinnerware. It is a precious time to create memories of home and family.

We used to have Thanksgiving, here at our house, with my parents as hosts. Mom would give me a shopping list. She would buy the turkey and I would get all the rest. We would have the same, familiar menu every Thanksgiving and we all looked forward to it with great anticipation.

It is important to plan ahead and save up for the special food we want to serve on holidays. This is the time for a little luxury and treats. I usually begin buying ingredients for Thanksgiving in October or the beginning of November. Still we must remember to make what we can afford. Holidays, birthdays, and other special occasions are wonderful times with the family.

Setting up Family Recipes

It was never common in our family to try out new recipes on a regular basis. We always made what was comforting and familiar. We supplement basic food with fresh produce and baked goods. The variety comes when there is a birthday or holiday celebration. On those occasions we serve special food. This is a more traditional method that has been going on for generations.

My mother made a homemade dinner for us each evening for all of our childhood years. She prepared the same, traditional food such as chicken with potatoes, spaghetti and meatballs, etc. We were thankful for her cooking and always looked forward to eating the food she carefully made with love. In her twilight years, my mother continued to make the same dinners for her and my father. Whenever I stopped in to visit in the early evening they would be at the table with one of Mother's comforting meals. Mom would welcome me and say, "Would you like some?" Dad's eyes would light up as he encouraged me to sit with them. I was grateful to hear my father's prayer and then I would enjoy the familiar food remembering long years ago. My parents were married for 50 years before they went home to heaven.

I have heard it commonly said by others such compliments as, "Nobody makes roast beef like my grandmother!" They love to remember the home cooking of much loved family members. These traditional dishes are made over and over again and enjoyed by all.

I keep my recipes in a large canister on the kitchen counter. These are handwritten and often include a little floral sticker to make it easy for me to find the most common recipes. When my children were growing up and I was not feeling well, I would say, "would you get the pizza recipe out of the canister and make dinner?" The children were always happy to do such important work. They would often return to my room to let me know the progress of their efforts. Sometimes they would say, "What do I do next?" In this way they learned to make the common foods of the household.

When I am doing the baking or cooking, I always take out one of these recipes even if I have the ingredients memorized. I use it as a reference so I don't forget any of the steps while I work. (You can see one of these recipe cards on page 94.)

Called to the Table

I have a little dinner bell stored on the hutch. When the grandchildren are visiting and a meal is ready, I will say to one of them, "It's time to ring the bell." The little child walks over and picks up the bell with a feeling of importance. The bell is rung to call the family to the table. All the children come running from the different rooms in the house. We do this for every snack and meal and the children love it.

When my children were young, they would be playing out on the property. When I finished making supper, I would go out on the front porch and ring a large bell which was attached to the wall of the house. This called all the children away from their play as they eagerly came "home" and into the house for a much anticipated meal.

The sound of the bell reminds me of church bells, calling people away from the toils of this life to a rest of worship and restoration. The evening meal can be a precious time of peace and togetherness.

When I was a child, my mother would walk into the living room and say, "Dinner is ready." We had been waiting to hear her voice. It was always comforting to know she had the food all ready for us. These days, as a mother and grandmother, I want my own children to remember my voice calling them to say, "Come on children, it's suppertime."

The Dinner Hour

This is the nicest part of the day! We have worked hard all day and are grateful to sit down together and enjoy a pleasant meal. In my childhood home, after Mother called us to the table, we would all sit down and have a quiet moment as we looked over at our Father. Dad would say the most wonderful prayer, asking a blessing on the food. He would thank the Lord for each of us and then close with a reverent and humble "Amen." The routine of hearing Dad's prayer was very comforting.

Part of the ceremony of dinner includes serving at the table. Does anyone need more milk? Would you like me to bring over the rest of the potatoes? Or, we need another place setting for Uncle Joe who just walked in the door. When we have a servant's heart, we enjoy taking care of everyone and making sure they are comfortable and happy as they eat.

A beautifully, yet humbly, set table is the training ground for good manners. We say "please" and "thank you." We keep our elbows off the table. We sit up straight and we look our best. Everyone has washed up before sitting down. It is a lovely time of fellowship and should include cheerful, uplifting conversation. This part of day is a quiet time. We are shut off from the world and all its cares. The phone is not in use. Business hours are over and it is time to enjoy a little rest with the family.

~ Comfort ~

"And the peace of God, which passeth all understanding, shall keep your hearts and minds through Christ Jesus."

Philippians 4:7

"I have been young, and now am old; yet have I not seen the righteous forsaken, nor his seed begging bread."

Psalm 37:25

"One thing have I desired of the Lord, that will I seek after; that I may dwell in the house of the Lord all the days of my life, to behold the beauty of the Lord, and to enquire in his temple."

Psalm 27:4

Serving in the Kitchen

~ Part 2 ~
Serving Meals & House Specials

Serving in the Kitchen

~ Sweet Hour of Prayer ~

Sweet Hour of Prayer! Sweet Hour of Prayer!

That calls me from a world of care,

And bids me at my Father's throne

Make all my wants and wishes known;

In seasons of distress and grief,

My soul has often found relief,

And oft escaped the tempter's snare

By thy return, sweet hour of prayer.

Hymn by William W. Walford, 1845

{Photograph on previous page: "Flowers on the table at our Home."}

Serving in the Kitchen

~ *Serving Meals & House Specials* ~

Breakfast, Lunch, and Dinner

(House Specials are menu selections you will commonly find at our house.)

Serving Breakfast – Menu Ideas

Menu 1
Homemade Muffin

Cantaloupe

Tea

Menu 2
Eggs, Sausage

Toast with Butter

Orange Juice or Coffee

Menu 3
Oatmeal

Grapefruit

Tea

Menu 4
Homemade Wheat Toast

Raspberry Jam

Orange Juice

Menu 5
Pancakes with Fresh Berries

Maple Syrup

Tea with Lemon

Serving in the Kitchen

Serving in the Kitchen

Breakfast in a rush: *From photograph on previous page*

When my son had to rush out the door for an appointment, I quickly made his breakfast while he got ready to leave. Since I was unsure of when he would be ready to eat, I set the table in a way to keep the food hot until he was able to eat.

In the photograph you will see a bowl with fruit, a cup, an empty plate, a fork and napkin, and some butter on a small plate. You will also see two dishes, used as serving bowls, with inverted plates to cover them. These covers will keep the food hot. The bowl contains eggs, cheese, and sausage. The covered plate holds hot toasted bread waiting to be buttered. He could then help himself by putting things on the empty plate.

After everything was prepared, I could walk away and go about the rest of my routine.

Serving in the Kitchen

Serving in the Kitchen

Breakfast on a tray table: *From photograph on previous page*

This is a simple meal of pancakes and maple syrup, served with tea and lemon. It is on a tray table in one of the bedrooms.

Serving in the Kitchen

Breakfast in a more formal style: *From photograph on previous page*

The table is set with a 10 ounce stainless steel teapot, a cup, bowl of oatmeal, plate with ½ grapefruit, and a napkin. The beautiful flowers and candle add a sense of warmth and beauty to an otherwise simple meal.

~ A Child's Prayer ~

God is great.

God is good.

Let us thank Him for our food.

By His hands we all are fed.

Give us, Lord, our Daily Bread.

Amen.

How to Pray

We pray before every meal.

We fold our hands.

We bow our heads.

We close our eyes.

We do this in reverent thanksgiving;

With gratefulness to God.

Serving Lunch – Menu Ideas

Menu 1
Grilled Cheese Sandwich
Pickles, Carrots
Milk or Juice

Menu 2
Vegetable Soup
Dinner Roll
Milk or Juice

Menu 3
Cheese Pizza
Fresh Fruit
Milk or Juice

Menu 4
Baked Potato with Olive Oil
Fresh Vegetables with Dinner Roll
Milk, Juice, or Ice Water

Menu 5
Spaghetti with Sauce
Garden Salad with Bread
Milk or Tea

Serving in the Kitchen

Serving in the Kitchen

Lunch with the family: *From photograph on previous page*

The table includes place settings for a baby and young child. You will see a plate on the highchair. There is a cloth napkin used as a placemat for a child's setting. This is intended to help keep the tablecloth clean.

Bowls of salad were made in advance and covered with plastic wrap before setting out on the table at each place. There are slices of bread on plates with plastic wrap over them, one for each section of the table.

Salt and pepper shakers, a bottle of salad dressing, and a canister of parmesan cheese have been set out.

Each place setting is supplied with silverware and a napkin.

The lunch to be served will be spaghetti with bread and salad.

Serving in the Kitchen

Serving in the Kitchen

Lunch with finger bowls: *From photograph on previous page*

When serving something that might be messy, such as something with sauce, it would save the need for extra napkins if we used little crystal finger bowls at each place setting. (Any 2 - ounce bowls will work nicely.) You just fill the bowl halfway full of water and set it above the plate on the table. Instruct children how to discreetly swish their fingers in the water and then dry them with their napkin.

This table setting includes a dinner bell. In the old days, in wealthy homes, the head of the table would ring the bell to call in a maid to wait on the table. We like to use our bell for fun. We use it to call the family to meals.

Serving in the Kitchen

Serving in the Kitchen

Lunch on a bed tray: *From photograph on previous page*

For a sick patient, a bed tray is the perfect option for serving a nice lunch. The patient could be propped up with pillows and enjoy her meal without having to go to the table.

This bed tray is covered with a cloth napkin. There is a bowl, a spoon, and a napkin. The lunch of crackers and soup is ready to be served.

Serving in the Kitchen

Lunch while on a picnic: *From photograph on previous page*

A simple lunch was packed into a pretty picnic purse. This is for dining on a patio table on the front porch of our home. There is a tablecloth on the table and napkins laid out.

The lunch is unpacked. It includes a sandwich wrapped in plastic wrap, chips and homemade cookies in plastic bags, and a bowl with freshly cut strawberries with a bit of whipped cream.

There are plastic spoons and forks available in the bag.

The lunch includes hot soup in a thermos.

Serving in the Kitchen

~ *Grandfather's Prayer* ~

Our Father, we thank you for your blessing. We thank you for loving us. We are so thankful to be able to be with our family gathered around the table to celebrate Thanksgiving with each other.

We love you Lord and ask you to bless our fellowship together today. We are so thankful for all the blessings you have given us.

We ask now that you bless this food and bless the hands that prepared it, and take a portion of it for the nourishment of our bodies and our souls in thy service.

In Jesus name we pray. Amen.

My father would say a prayer like this before every Thanksgiving dinner. On his last Thanksgiving with us, I made sure this prayer was written down so we could always have it. His voice, and his heartfelt love for the Lord, comforted us all.

Serving in the Kitchen

Serving Dinner – Menu Ideas

Menu 1
Beef Stew

Whole Wheat Biscuits

Milk or Tea

Menu 2
Fettuccini Alfredo

Broccoli, Peas, and Challah Bread

Milk or Juice

Menu 3
Cheese Lasagna

Salad and Italian Bread

Milk or Juice

Menu 4
Hamburger / Vegetable Soup

Mashed Potatoes and Bread

Milk, Tea, or Ice Water

Menu 5
Baked Chicken with Stuffing

Baked Potatoes and Corn

Coffee or Tea

Serving in the Kitchen

Serving in the Kitchen

Dinner on a holiday: *From photograph on previous page*

This picture is for our Thanksgiving dinner. There is a cloth napkin at each place setting. A pretty candle lights up the atmosphere with warmth and comfort.

An antique gravy boat on a stand sits in the middle of the table. This was passed down to me from my mother and grandmother. I set it out every year on Thanksgiving.

For serving on this holiday, the turkey will be brought over, already sliced, on a platter. The mashed potatoes and other dishes will soon be set up in the middle of the table. Extra portions are kept on the stove or on the sideboard table.

Serving in the Kitchen

Dinner for the family: *From photograph on previous page*

There is a pretty tablecloth set out to bring a sense of beauty to the meal. Homemade cloth napkins and silverware are at each place setting.

I used a casserole pan as a serving dish to hold the Fettuccini. Later, the lid can cover this and it will be stored in the refrigerator. There is enough to provide lunches for a few days. There is a small plate beside the casserole pan for the serving fork.

For this meal, each plate is carefully portioned out by the hostess and then the family is called to the table.

You might also notice there are crystal finger bowls at each place setting to add a sense of luxury, as well as convenience, to the table.

This is a simple meal of Fettuccini noodles with broccoli, peas, challah bread and butter. It is presented in a formal way to bring grace and happiness to the family.

Serving in the Kitchen

Serving in the Kitchen

Dinner for two: *From photograph on previous page*

The table is set in the early evening. There is an old white lace tablecloth for a cover. Flameless candles and plastic flowers decorate the center.

A glass of ice water will be placed beside each plate.

This will be a more casual meal. The food will soon be brought over. It will be a light and peaceful dinner.

~ A Servant's Heart ~

"Wherefore comfort yourselves together, and edify one another, even as also ye do."

I Thessalonians 5:11

"And whatsoever ye do, do it heartily, as to the Lord, and not unto men."

Colossians 3:23

"Serve the Lord with gladness: come before his presence with singing."

Psalm 100:2

". . . but as for me and my house, we will serve the Lord."

Joshua 24:15

Serving in the Kitchen

~ *Part 3*~
Recipes

Serving in the Kitchen

~ *What a Friend We Have in Jesus* ~

What a Friend we have in Jesus,

All our sins and griefs to bear!

What a privilege to carry

Everything to God in prayer!

O what peace we often forfeit,

O what needless pain we bear,

All because we do not carry

Everything to God in prayer!

Hymn by Joseph Scriven, 1855

{Photograph on previous page: "Flowers on the table at our Home."}

Serving in the Kitchen

~ Recipes ~

A Sampler of Recipes from My Kitchen

Serving in the Kitchen

> **Recipe for Cleaning the Kitchen**
>
> Estimated time: 30 minutes.
>
> Dry any dishes in drainer and put them away.
>
> Empty the sink and wash it.
>
> Load the sink with hot, soapy water and dishes.
>
> Clean off the counters. Wash and dry them.
>
> Sweep the floor.
>
> Wash all the dishes (from all rooms).
>
> Scrub the stove and sink.
>
> Enjoy a good rest!

{Photograph on previous page: "A bookcase in our guest room used as a pantry."}

Serving in the Kitchen

Hamburger and Vegetable Soup over Mashed Potatoes

Serving in the Kitchen

Hamburger and Vegetable Soup over Mashed Potatoes

10.5 ounce can of condensed vegetable soup plus one can of water
1 pound ground turkey burger or ground hamburger
5 pounds of potatoes (plus milk, butter, salt and pepper as desired)

A

Peel and cut the potatoes, placing them in a large pot. Bring to a boil. Then turn down to medium heat. Continue to boil on medium for about 25 to 30 minutes, stirring occasionally.

B

While the potatoes are cooking, start frying the burger in a large frying pan. Cook completely until well browned.

C

Add the can of vegetable soup to the cooked burger in the frying pan. Add one can of water to this. Stir all together with a spatula. Bring to a boil. Then turn down to medium low heat to simmer while the potatoes finish cooking. Stir occasionally with spatula.

When the potatoes are finished, there are two options for preparing them:

Option one (classic version) -

Drain the potatoes into a colander in the sink. Return the potatoes to the pan. Add a small amount of butter (about 1 teaspoon) and milk (1/4 cup or more) as you mash them up with a potato masher. Add more milk, in small amounts, as needed to reach desired consistency. Add salt and pepper, as desired, and stir it all together. Place a cover on the pan to keep potatoes hot until ready to serve.

Option two (no butter or milk version) -

Place a medium sized bowl in the sink. Place a colander over this. Put the cooked potatoes into the colander to drain. The potato broth will fill up the bowl underneath. Return the potatoes to the pan. Use the potato broth instead of milk when mashing the potatoes.

Serving:

Place burger / vegetable mixture into a serving dish. Place potatoes in a serving bowl. Bring these to the table.

Place a portion of mashed potatoes on each plate.

Use a ladle to serve the burger / vegetable mixture. Top this onto the potatoes. Serve with bread.

Serving in the Kitchen

Whole Wheat Molasses Bread

Serving in the Kitchen

Whole Wheat Molasses Bread

A

2 cups white flour
2 teaspoons salt
1 Tablespoon sugar
3 teaspoons active dry yeast

B

2 cups very warm water

C

2 Tablespoons olive oil
2 Tablespoons molasses

D

3 cups wheat flour (plus ½ cup)

Take a large stainless steel bowl and rinse in hot water to heat it up. Quickly dry the bowl with a kitchen towel. Do the same with a glass measuring cup. Then measure out the ingredients in (A) and put in the bowl. Stir until mixed.

Pour the warm water (from B) into the bowl. (It should bubble up because of the yeast.) Stir this together. Then add the olive oil and molasses (from C). Stir until well mixed.

Slowly add 1 cup of flour from (D) mixing it together. Then add another cup and continue to stir. Add another cup of flour. Set aside ½ cup of flour to use during the kneading process.

Serving in the Kitchen

While the dough is still in the bowl, pour a little olive oil on top of the dough. Coat your hand with a little flour and start doing the kneading a few times. This will make the dough easier to work with and less sticky on the counter.

Place the dough on floured counter and knead for about 3 minutes. Add some of the additional flour as needed. Continue to knead, adding a little of the flour, until the dough is a smooth ball.

Put a little olive oil on the bottom of the stainless steel bowl. Place the dough in the bowl and then turn it over to coat with the oil.

Cover the bowl with a cloth or plastic wrap. Allow to rise until doubled in size, about an hour.

[The dough will rise best in a warm environment. One way to do this: Preheat oven to 200 degrees. Once the oven reaches that temperature, shut it off. Meanwhile, boil a little water on the stove. Take a round cake pan (about 8 x 8 or so in size). Fill this pan halfway full with the boiling water. Place this pan on the lower rack of the oven. Put the stainless steel bowl, with the dough in it, on the top rack of the oven. This method will keep it warm and help it to rise.]

I take whatever flour is left on the counter and put it into a small bowl with a lid. I use it later for rolling out the dough. In this way, the kitchen is clean and the counters are tidy, while we wait for the dough to rise.

Once the dough has risen, lightly punch it down in the middle. Then place it on a floured counter. Cut dough in half.

Lightly grease 2 loaf pans. (Size: 9 x 5 inch.)

Using a rolling pin, roll out one of the doughs into a rectangle shape, around 9 inches by 10 inches. From the long side of the dough, roll the dough tightly like a jelly roll. Pinch the edges and seam to hold the dough firmly in place.

Place the rolled dough into a loaf pan with the seam side down.

Quickly insert a fork into the dough a couple of times.

Repeat process with the second dough.

Allow the dough to rise again, for about an hour.

To Bake:

Preheat oven to 425 degrees.

Place the loaf pans into the oven and bake for 20 to 24 minutes. (Oven temperatures vary. Start checking the bread after 20 minutes to avoid having the crust burn from overcooking.)

Once these are finished baking, remove from the stove and allow to sit for about 5 minutes.

Then transfer the loaves to a cooling rack. Allow to cool completely before cutting. It is best to wait a few hours before cutting in order to prevent crumbling of the crust in the cutting process.

To Store:

Use a bread bag or gallon sized Ziploc bag to store the loaves. The loaves can either be stored whole or in slices.

Freezing Bread:

You can put sliced bread into a gallon sized freezer bag and store in the freezer. Simply take out a piece of bread as needed. These slices can be toasted in a toaster oven and spread with jam or butter.

Cinnamon Bread Option:

Make one loaf regular wheat bread and the second loaf cinnamon bread by making a slight variation in the directions.

Roll out the second dough into a rectangular shape. Let sit while you prepare the cinnamon filling:

Filling:

2 Tablespoons honey

1 teaspoon cinnamon

Put the honey in a small saucepan. Add the cinnamon. Turn the heat on low and stir constantly until the cinnamon is dissolved. Remove from heat.

Use a Tablespoon to spread the cinnamon mixture over the center of the dough. Leave at least one inch untouched on all sides. Roll the dough, tightly, like a jelly roll. Then continue with normal directions.

Once the bread dough is placed in a pan, use a sharp knife to slash a line down the center of the dough to differentiate it from the regular loaf of wheat bread.

Serving in the Kitchen

Cheese Lasagna

Serving in the Kitchen

Cheese Lasagna

15 ounce tub of ricotta cheese
29 ounce can of tomato sauce
1 pound box of lasagna noodles
2 cups (16 ounce) mozzarella cheese (Using ½ for the layers and ½ for the top)

Boil the noodles according to package instructions. Then drain and rinse with cold water in order to cool the noodles down for easier handling.

In a large stainless steel bowl, mix tub of ricotta cheese with ¾ of the can of tomato sauce. Stir this together until well mixed.

Begin layering the lasagna:

A

From the ¼ amount of tomato sauce which is remaining, spread small amount (approximately 2 to 3 Tablespoons) of it on the bottom of a 13 x 9 inch pan.

B

Place 3 lasagna noodles for the first layering.

C

Top each noodle with one heaping Tablespoon of the ricotta mixture, then spread it over the noodles. Next, sprinkle mozzarella cheese over it sparingly.

D

Repeat steps (B) and (C) until you get to 3 remaining noodles.

E

Place the last 3 noodles on top. Cover these with the rest of the tomato sauce and the last ½ of the mozzarella cheese.

Put a cover on the pan and store it in the refrigerator. I normally prepare this the day before I plan to serve it for dinner. (Be sure to remove the cover before baking.)

Bake in a preheated 350 degree oven for approximately 45 minutes.

Once the lasagna is taken out of the oven, allow to sit for about 5 minutes. Then take a pizza cutter to divide up the lasagna. You should be able to cut it twice, between the noodles, horizontally. Then about 4 times vertically. This should provide you with about 8 servings. Use a spatula to remove each piece to serve.

Serving in the Kitchen

Beef Stew

Serving in the Kitchen

Beef Stew

A

2 Tablespoons vegetable oil
1 pound beef stew meat

B

3 Tablespoons white flour
5 cups warm water

C

1.5 ounce packet of beef stew seasoning mix

D

4 to 5 pounds of potatoes
1 pound carrots

Using the ingredients in (A), put the vegetable oil in a frying pan. Turn heat on to medium and add the beef. Brown for a few minutes. Remove beef from pan. Cut into very small pieces and then return it to the pan. Fry until meat is well done.

In a 6 quart stockpot, put the meat and drippings. Add the flour from (B) and stir until meat is well coated. Add the warm water. Stir all together. Bring to a boil. Then add the seasoning mix from (C). Stir until dissolved.

Bring back to a boil. Then turn heat down to low. Cover and cook (with a low boil) for one hour. Stir occasionally with a spatula so you are able to regularly scrape the bottom of the pan. (This will prevent the stew from sticking and burning the pan.)

Serving in the Kitchen

About 20 - 30 minutes before the hour is up, begin peeling and cutting the vegetables in (D). Place these in a colander or large bowl.

When the hour is up, pour the potatoes and carrots into the stockpot. Carefully stir these until they are coated with the broth. Bring back to a boil. Keep a good watch on this and continue to stir often until the vegetables start to cook down to fit better in the pan. Then turn heat down to a low boil. Cover and cook for 45 minutes. Continue to stir occasionally with a spatula.

When the cooking time is complete, it is okay to continue cooking for another 10 minutes or so. Keep a cover on the pan while you prepare to serve.

Serve with homemade biscuits or bread.

Serving in the Kitchen

Whole Wheat Biscuits

Serving in the Kitchen

Whole Wheat Biscuits

A

1 cup white flour
1 cup wheat flour
2 and ½ teaspoons baking powder
¾ teaspoon salt

B

¼ cup vegetable shortening

C

1 cup fat free buttermilk

D

¼ cup white flour

In a large stainless steel bowl, mix together all the ingredients from (A). Add the shortening from (B) into the bowl. Use a fork (or pastry cutter) to press down on the shortening into the flour mixture. Mix and continue to press the shortening with a fork until it is incorporated into the mix.

Add the buttermilk from (C) into the mixture. Stir this all together.

Take the flour from (D) and put into a small bowl. Use this while kneading and rolling out the dough.

Sprinkle a little flour on the counter. Take the biscuit dough from the bowl and begin kneading. Add a little flour while you work. When the dough is smooth, begin to roll it out.

Roll the dough about ¼ to ½ an inch thick, depending on your preference (I like to do thinner, flat biscuits). Use a floured, round cookie cutter, or biscuit cutter, to cut out the biscuits. (If you don't have a cookie cutter, you can use the top of a small cup.) Place on an ungreased, non-stick, cookie sheet.

Note: I often stop at this point and put plastic wrap over the cookie sheet. Then I put the pan of unbaked biscuits in the refrigerator. By doing this early in the day, it is easier to bake them later on just before a meal is ready. With this method they will be hot and fresh with little effort.

To Bake:

Bake in a pre-heated 450 degree oven for 10 to 12 minutes. Serve hot with butter. Save any remaining biscuits in an airtight container or a sealed plastic bag.

Additional Baking and Serving Suggestions

- Serve biscuits with eggs for breakfast.
- Offer biscuits on the side of lunch or dinner.
- Serve biscuits with jam for a snack.
- *Pizza*: Reserve ¼ of the biscuit dough for a thin pizza crust. Use an 8 or 9 inch cake pan. Roll out the dough to fit the pan. Preheat the oven to 450 degrees. Bake the crust for 2 minutes. Then remove from the oven. Add sauce and cheese. Then bake for about 8 to 12 minutes.
- *Baked Apple Treat:* Take 2 small pieces of biscuit dough. Top one with sliced apples, cinnamon, and a drizzle of honey. Cover with the 2nd piece of dough. Pinch edges all around to seal. Insert a fork into the dough to make a few little holes. Bake at 450 degrees for 8 to 12 minutes, or until the crust is nicely browned.

Serving in the Kitchen

Simple Vegetable Soup

Serving in the Kitchen

Serving in the Kitchen

Simple Vegetable Soup

A

3 or 4 medium potatoes
3 carrots
4 cups water
Dash of salt and pepper
1 teaspoon olive oil

B

1 clove garlic

Peel and cut potatoes and carrots from (A) and put into a medium saucepan. Add the water, salt, pepper and olive oil. Bring to a boil. Then turn down to medium, low heat. Stir occasionally. Cook for 31 minutes. Then turn it down to simmer.

Peel and cut one clove of garlic from (B) into a few pieces. Place in a blender. Take 1 and ½ ladles of the soup, including some of the broth from it, into the blender with the garlic. Blend well for several seconds. Then pour this into the pan, stirring it in with the soup. This will create a "creamy" consistency.

Serving Size:

Small serving size is 1 ladle, or about ½ cup. Serve with saltine crackers.

Serving in the Kitchen

Saving the soup:

Once the soup cools, store in a plastic bowl with lid in the refrigerator, for up to 4 days.

{Photograph above: "An old chalkboard next to my kitchen, announcing the lunch menu for the day."}

Serving in the Kitchen

Fettuccini Alfredo with Broccoli

Serving in the Kitchen

Fettuccini Alfredo with Broccoli

1 pound box of fettuccini noodles
14.5 ounce jar of Alfredo sauce
2 cups frozen broccoli florets

A

Begin preparing the fettuccini noodles as directed on package.

B

While the noodles are cooking, get out a medium sized pot. Put in 4 cups of water. Bring water to a boil.

Add in 2 cups of frozen broccoli florets. Bring back to a boil.

Reduce heat to medium low.

Cook for about 13 minutes, or according to package directions.

Drain out the water through a colander. Return broccoli to the pan.

Use a fork and butter knife to cut the broccoli into smaller pieces. Set aside.

C

After the noodles have finished cooking, drain the water through a colander.

Return noodles to the pan.

Pour the jar of Alfredo sauce in with the noodles. (There is no need to heat up the sauce.) Stir well.

D

Add the cut broccoli in with the noodles. Stir this all together.

Serve warm with peas and challah bread.

Challah Bread

Serving in the Kitchen

Serving in the Kitchen

Challah Bread

A

2 cups white flour
1/3 cup white sugar
1 teaspoon salt
3 teaspoons active dry yeast

B

2 cups very warm water

C

¼ cup olive oil
1 egg (well beaten with a fork)

D

3 and ½ cups of white flour

E

½ to 1 cup of additional white flour

Take a large stainless steel bowl and rinse it in hot water to heat it up. Quickly dry the bowl. Do the same with a glass measuring cup. Put all ingredients from (A) into the bowl.

Then measure out the water in (B) and put in the bowl. Stir this all together.

In a small bowl, beat the egg from (C). Pour this into the stainless steel bowl. Then add the olive oil from (C) to the mixture. Stir all together.

Add two cups of the flour from (D) to the mixture. Stir together. Add more of the flour to the mixture (about ½ cup at a time) until it forms a dough. Pour a small amount of olive oil over the dough to make it easier to work with.

Set aside the flour from (E) to use during the kneading and rolling process.

Place dough onto a floured surface and knead for about 3 minutes. Add flour as necessary. Continue to knead the dough until it forms a soft ball. (It may be a little sticky.)

Once the dough is ready, put a little olive oil in the stainless steel bowl. Place the dough on top of this and turn it over a few times to coat it with oil.

Cover the dough (with plastic wrap over the bowl) and let rise until doubled in size, about one hour.

The dough will rise best in a warm environment. One way to do this is: Preheat oven to 200 degrees. Once the oven reaches that temperature, shut it off. Meanwhile, boil a little water on the stove. Take a round cake pan (about 8 x 8 or so in size). Fill this pan halfway full with the boiling water. Place this pan on the lower rack of the oven. Put the stainless steel bowl with the dough in it, on the top rack of the oven. This will keep it warm and help it to rise.

Get 2 cookie sheets ready. (Size: 15 x 10 inch non-stick pans.)

Once the dough has finished the rising process, remove it from the bowl. Put it on a floured surface and cut the dough in half.

Put a little olive oil in the stainless steel bowl. Coat the 2 doughs in the oil. Then place them back onto a floured surface.

Cut each half into six pieces. You should now have a total of 12 pieces.

Roll each piece by hand into a 14 inch rope. This should give you 12 ropes of dough.

Take 3 ropes and braid. Pinch ends to seal. This makes the bottom of the 1st loaf. Place this on one of the cookie sheets.

Take 3 ropes and braid. Pinch ends to seal. This makes the bottom of the 2nd loaf. Place this on the other cookie sheet.

Take 3 ropes and braid. Pinch ends to seal. This makes the top of the 1st loaf. Place this on top of one of the doughs on the cookie sheet. Pinch sides and edges to seal the doughs together.

Take 3 ropes and braid. Pinch ends to seal. This makes the top of the 2nd loaf. Place this on top of the other dough on the cookie sheet. Pinch sides and edges to seal the doughs together. Then take a fork and insert it a few times into each loaf.

The oven should still be a little bit warm. It should not be on. Place the cookie sheets into this oven and allow the dough to rise until it doubles in size. It should take about an hour.

After the dough is ready, carefully remove the pans from the oven. Place them on the stove top to wait.

Preheat the oven to 375 degrees.

When the oven reaches the desired temperature, put the two pans in the oven. Bake the breads for around 20 to 30 minutes until they are nicely browned.

Remove the pans from the oven. Allow to sit for about 5 minutes.

Optional: For a soft, delicious crust, butter the tops and sides of the loaves.*

Transfer loaves to a cooling rack. Allow to cool completely before cutting.

To store the bread:

You can cut the loaves into slices. Place wax paper into a couple of gallon sized bags. Put the pieces of bread into these bags and seal to close. Remove bread to serve whenever needed.

Serving in the Kitchen

Refrigerator Baked Potatoes

Serving in the Kitchen

Refrigerator Baked Potatoes

5 pounds of potatoes

To Cook:

A

Preheat oven to 350 degrees. Gather and wash the potatoes. Lay these out on a large cookie sheet lined with aluminum foil. Take a fork and insert it a few times in each potato. Then bake them for about 90 minutes.

Remove the pan from the oven. Allow to cool for about 30 minutes. Then store potatoes in a gallon size freezer bag in the refrigerator for up to 4 days.

Serving size is one potato per person.

B

Preparing cooked potatoes:

Take potato out of the bag. Use a paring knife to remove peel. Then cut the potato in half before cutting it in thin slices.

Serving Suggestions:

Lunch

Warm the potato in a toaster oven or microwave.

Toaster oven: Put the sliced potato on a pan lined with aluminum foil. Bake at 350 degrees for about 5 to 8 minutes or until heated through.

Serving in the Kitchen

Microwave: Put the potato on a microwave-safe plate. Cover with a paper towel. Set for about one minute.

Take the heated potato and put it on a serving plate. Drizzle with olive oil. Serve with a dinner roll, sliced fresh carrots, and assorted sliced vegetables such as radishes, celery, cucumber, and lettuce. (Any fresh vegetables you have available will work well.) Serve with salt and pepper if desired.

Other suggested options:

After step (A) and (B):

<u>Breakfast</u>

Fry the potatoes and serve with eggs and toast for breakfast.

<u>Dinner</u>

Add warmed potatoes to pasta for a filling meal. Or serve potatoes as a side dish to go with chicken and corn or peas.

Serving in the Kitchen

Homemade Frozen Pizzas

Serving in the Kitchen

Serving in the Kitchen

Homemade Frozen Pizzas

A

2 cups wheat flour
1 teaspoon salt
1 teaspoon sugar
    ½ teaspoon garlic powder (optional)
    ½ teaspoon onion powder (optional)
    ½ teaspoon dried basil (optional)
    ½ teaspoon dried oregano (optional)
1 teaspoon active dry yeast

B

1 and ½ cups very warm water

C

1 Tablespoon Olive Oil (plus extra)

D

2 cups white flour (plus extra)

E

15 ounce can of plain tomato sauce
16 ounces of Mozzarella cheese

Preheat oven to 450 degrees.

Start by warming a large stainless steel bowl. Just use hot water and rinse it off for a minute or so in the sink. (Using a hot bowl is important to keep the ingredients at a consistent warm temperature.) Quickly dry the bowl with a dish towel.

Combine together all the ingredients from (A) into the bowl.

Take a glass measuring cup and rinse it off with hot water to get it warm. Then quickly dry the cup.

Measure out 1 and ½ cups of hot water (B) from the sink and add it to the bowl. This should cause the ingredients to bubble up, which means the yeast is working.

Stir this all together.

Then add 1 Tablespoon of olive oil (C). Stir in a cup of the white flour (D).

Then stir in the remaining flour.

Put a little flour on your hand. Then "squish" the dough a few times, while still in the bowl, to form it into a less-sticky, workable dough.

Place about ½ cup of additional flour into a small bowl. You will need this as you do the kneading and rolling of the dough.

Put the dough on a floured surface and begin to knead.

Add a little more white flour as you work.

Knead for about 4 or 5 minutes until the dough forms a soft ball.

Then pour a little olive oil in the stainless steel bowl. Coat the dough in the oiled bowl and allow to rest for a few minutes.

On a floured surface, cut the dough into 8 equal size pieces.

Lightly grease two 8 or 9 inch cake pans.

Roll out one of the doughs with a rolling pin. Form into a circle that will fit the cake pan.

Place the dough into the pan. Repeat with another dough.

We are going to "pre-bake" the dough to make pizza crusts.

Bake in a preheated 450 degree oven for 2 minutes. Remove the pans from the oven.

Allow the crusts to cool in the pans for about 3 minutes.

Cut 8 pieces of wax paper, large enough to set the crusts on. Put these on the kitchen table. Then transfer each cooled crust onto the wax paper.

Repeat the process of rolling out the remainder of doughs and baking and cooling them.

Once all the crusts are on the wax paper, top each crust with tomato sauce. Then sprinkle a small amount of cheese on each crust. (E)

When each pizza is ready, cover each one with another piece of wax paper.

Fold down the wax paper on all sides to make it easy to slide into a freezer bag.

You can store 2 - 3 of these pizzas in a gallon size, Ziploc freezer bag.

Serving in the Kitchen

Store the pizzas in the freezer.

To Cook:

Preheat oven to 450 degrees. Remove pizza from freezer bag. Remove wax paper. Place pizza in a cake pan or on a cookie sheet. Bake for about 10 to 12 minutes. Serve hot.

Serving in the Kitchen

Italian Bread

Serving in the Kitchen

Italian Bread

A

2 cups white flour
2 and ¼ teaspoons active dry yeast
2 teaspoons salt
1 Tablespoon sugar

B

1 Tablespoon olive oil
1 and ¾ cups very warm water

C

3 additional cups of white flour

D

A small amount of cornmeal (optional) for the bottom of the pan.

Take a large stainless steel bowl and rinse in hot water to heat it up. Do the same with a glass measuring cup. Quickly dry these with a kitchen towel.

Then measure out the ingredients in (A) and put in the bowl. Stir until mixed.

Pour the warm water (from B) into the bowl. (It should bubble up because of the yeast.) Stir this together.

Then add the olive oil (from B).

Stir until well mixed.

Slowly add 1 cup of flour from (C) mixing it together. Then add another cup and continue to stir. (Set aside the 3rd cup of flour to use during the kneading process.)

Put a little flour on your hand. Then "squish" the dough a few times, while still in the bowl, to form it into a less-sticky, workable dough.

Place the dough on floured counter and knead for about 3 to 4 minutes. Add some of the additional flour as needed.

Continue to knead, adding a little of the flour, until the dough is a smooth ball.

Put a little olive oil on the bottom of the stainless steel bowl. Place the dough in the bowl and then turn it over a few times to coat with oil.

Cover the bowl with a cloth or plastic wrap.

Let sit for 20 to 30 minutes.

Get 2 cookie sheets ready. (Size: 15 x 10 inch non-stick pans.) Lightly grease them.

(*Optional suggestion* (D): Lightly sprinkle the bottom of the pans with cornmeal.)

Remove the dough from the bowl. Cut the dough into two equal size pieces.

Put a little more olive oil in the bowl. Coat each dough in the oil.

Using a rolling pin, roll out one of the doughs into a rectangle shape, around 14 inches by 10 inches.

From the long side of the dough, roll the dough tightly like a jelly roll.

Serving in the Kitchen

Pinch the edges and seam to hold the dough firmly in place.

Place the rolled dough onto the cookie sheet, with the seam side down.

Quickly insert a fork into the dough a couple of times.

Wrap the dough with a little plastic wrap.

Repeat process with the second dough.

Place both pans of dough in the refrigerator for about 2 hours.

When the dough is ready, preheat the oven to 425 degrees.

Remove the pans from the refrigerator.

Allow to sit on the counter for about 15 minutes.

Just before baking, use a sharp knife to quickly slash a straight line down the center of the dough or slice a few diagonal lines down the top of the dough.

Then put the pans in the oven.

Bake for about 20 to 25 minutes.

Remove pans from oven.

Let sit for about 5 minutes.

Transfer bread to a wire cooling rack.

(*Optional*: Brush the top and sides of the bread with butter. I use a sandwich bag as a glove and take a small amount of butter to spread over the bread.)

Allow to cool for about 15 minutes before cutting. This tastes best when served warm.

Serving in the Kitchen

Chocolate Chip Oat Muffins

Serving in the Kitchen

Chocolate Chip Oat Muffins

2 cups all purpose flour
2/3 cup light brown sugar (lightly packed)
½ teaspoon salt
2 teaspoons baking powder
2 cups oats (Quaker finely cut – 1 minute oats)

Wet ingredients:

1 egg (beat well)
¾ cup of apple juice
¾ cup of water
1 teaspoon vanilla extract
½ cup margarine (one stick)
½ cup (4 ounces) semi-sweet chocolate chips (or mini chocolate chips)

Preheat oven to 400 degrees.

Grease a 12 cup muffin pan. Melt the butter in a small saucepan on low heat. Then set it aside to cool.

You will need 2 separate bowls: one for the wet ingredients and one for the dry ingredients.

Mix together the flour, brown sugar, salt, and baking powder. Add the oats and stir until well mixed. Make a well in the center of the ingredients and set aside.

In another bowl, beat the egg. Add the apple juice, water, vanilla extract, and butter. Stir well.

Pour the wet ingredients into the bowl of dry ingredients.

Serving in the Kitchen

Stir a few times until combined. (Do not over-mix.)

Then add the chocolate chips. Stir just until mixed.

Scoop the batter into the muffin cups.

Bake for 20 to 25 minutes.

Remove pan from oven and let sit for 10 minutes.

Remove muffins from pan, placing them on a wire cooling rack.

Serve warm or allow to cool completely before storing them in an airtight container.

Serving in the Kitchen

Cinnamon Applesauce Cake

Serving in the Kitchen

Serving in the Kitchen

Cinnamon Applesauce Cake

A

1 cup white flour
1 cup wheat flour
¾ cup light brown sugar (lightly packed)
2 teaspoons baking powder
1 teaspoon salt
1 teaspoon cinnamon

B

1 cup apple juice
¼ cup water
1 Tablespoon applesauce (unsweetened)
1 Tablespoon olive oil
1 egg (beaten)

C   (*Prepare Optional Topping*)

¼ cup white flour
½ teaspoon cinnamon
1/3 cup brown sugar
2 Tablespoons margarine

In a medium sized bowl, mix together the first three ingredients from (C). Stir until well mixed. Then add the margarine. Using a fork, push it flat against the margarine over and over again to mix it into the rest of the ingredients. (This is much like one would do when using a pastry cutter.) Continue to do this, moving the fork around to different areas of the ingredients until the mixture resembles a crumbly texture. This will be the streusel topping.

Preheat the oven to 350 degrees.

In a large stainless steel bowl, mix together all the ingredients in (A). In a separate bowl, mix together the ingredients in (B). Set aside.

Take the ingredients from (B) and pour them into the stainless steel bowl with the ingredients from (A). Stir together for about 1 to 2 minutes until well blended.

To Bake:

Grease a square cake pan (9 x 9 inch).

Pour the batter (from the stainless steel bowl) into the cake pan.

> (*Add Optional Topping*)
>
> Using a teaspoon, loosely sprinkle the topping (from C) mixture evenly over the top of the batter.

Bake for 40 - 45 minutes.

Allow to cool at least 15 minutes before cutting. After it has cooled completely, store the pieces of cake in an airtight container lined with wax paper.

> *Note*: When you make this cake with the optional topping, it becomes a traditional coffee cake.

Serving in the Kitchen

Oatmeal Chocolate Chip Cookies

Serving in the Kitchen

Serving in the Kitchen

Oatmeal Chocolate Chip Cookies

A

1 and ½ cups white flour
1 teaspoon baking soda
¼ teaspoon salt

B

1 cup light brown sugar (lightly packed)
1 cup margarine (2 sticks)
1 teaspoon pure vanilla extract
1 egg

C

2 cups quick cooking oats (Quaker 1 minute oats)

D

1/2 cup (4 ounces) semi-sweet chocolate chips

Preheat oven to 350 degrees.

Put all the ingredients from (A) into a small bowl, stir together, then set aside. Measure out the oats from (C) and set aside.

Details for (B) – In a small saucepan, heat up about 1 cup of water to boiling. Then pour out the water into the sink in order to empty the pan (or use the hot water to make a cup of tea). (The pan is now hot enough to quickly melt the margarine.) Put the margarine inside the hot pan. Take a butter knife to cut the 2 sticks up into smaller pieces so they will melt faster. Then set the pan aside so the melted margarine will cool.

Serving in the Kitchen

Beat the egg in a small bowl. Add the vanilla extract.

Put the brown sugar in a large bowl. Add the egg and vanilla mixture, then add the melted margarine. Stir this all together until well mixed. Pour in all the ingredients from (A). Mix this all together with a large, sturdy spoon. Then stir for a few more minutes.

Carefully stir in the oats from (C). Then stir in the chocolate chips from (D).

To Bake:

Use an ice cream scoop or teaspoon to measure out the dough. (Try to have each cookie the same size.) Drop each scoop of dough onto an ungreased, non-stick cookie sheet. You should be able to space these out in the pan to have one dozen per batch. Bake for about 13 - 14 minutes. Then remove pan from oven. Let sit for 2 minutes. Then, using a spatula, transfer each cookie to a cooling rack. Allow to cool for about 4 minutes. Then store in an airtight container lined with wax paper.

Repeat until all dough has been used.

Serving size is one.

If you have two, that's okay.

If you have three, stop and save some for another day.

Serving in the Kitchen

Olive Oil Cookies

Serving in the Kitchen

Olive Oil Cookies

A

2 and ½ cups white flour
½ teaspoon salt
1 teaspoon baking soda

B

¾ cup olive oil
¼ cup water
1 cup light brown sugar (lightly packed)
½ cup white sugar
1 teaspoon vanilla extract

C

2 eggs (well beaten with a fork)

D

½ cup oats (Quaker quick cooking 1 minute oats)
¾ cup semi-sweet chocolate chips

Preheat oven to 375 degrees.

In a small bowl, mix together ingredients in (A). Then set it aside.

In a large bowl, mix together the ingredients in (B). Add the eggs from (C). Mix well. Then add ingredients from (A). Stir all together with a sturdy spoon.

Then stir in the oats from (D). Stir well.

Stir in the chocolate chips from (D).

To Bake:

Use an ice cream scoop or teaspoon to measure out the dough. (Try to have each cookie the same size.)

Drop each scoop of dough onto a lightly greased cookie sheet. (Size: 15 x 10 inch non-stick pans.)

You should be able to space these out in the pan to have one dozen per batch.

Bake for about 12 - 14 minutes.

Then remove pan from oven. Let sit for 2 minutes.

Then, using a spatula, transfer each cookie to a cooling rack.

Allow to cool for about 4 minutes. Then store in an airtight container lined with wax paper.

Repeat until all dough has been used.

Serving size is one cookie.

> These cookies are expensive to make because of the cost of the olive oil.
>
> They are a rare treat.

Serving in the Kitchen

Mini Chocolate Chip Cookies

Serving in the Kitchen

Mini Chocolate Chip Cookies

A

2 and ½ cups white flour
1 teaspoon baking soda
½ teaspoon salt

B

1 cup (2 sticks) gently melted margarine
1 cup light brown sugar (lightly packed)
½ cup white sugar
1 teaspoon vanilla extract

C

2 eggs (beaten)

D

½ cup oats (Quaker 1 minute, quick oats)
¾ cup semi-sweet mini chocolate chips

Preheat the oven to 375 degrees.

To melt the margarine from (B), take a small pan with about 1 cup of water. Bring to a boil. Then discard the water in the sink (or use the hot water to make a cup of tea). Put the margarine in the empty pan. The heated pan will melt the margarine at a gentle pace. Take a butter knife and cut the sticks of margarine into smaller pieces. Then set the pan aside as the margarine will continue to melt on its own.

In a medium sized bowl, mix together the ingredients in (A). Set aside.

Serving in the Kitchen

In a large stainless steel bowl, mix together the ingredients in (B). Add the margarine. Stir this all together until well mixed.

In a small bowl, beat the two eggs. Set aside.

Measure out the oats and mini chocolate chips from (D). Set aside.

In the large stainless steel bowl, add the beaten eggs from (C) to the mixture of (B). Stir this all together.

Then add the ingredients from (A) into the large bowl. Stir until well mixed.

Then stir in the oats and mini chocolate chips.

Set up two ungreased, non-stick, cookie sheets.

Use two teaspoons to measure out the cookie dough onto the pans. Use one spoon to scoop out the dough. The second spoon will help move it onto the pan. This should produce about 3 and ½ dozen small cookies.

Bake 10 to 12 minutes.

When the cookies come out of the oven, allow to cool in the pan for 2 minutes. Then transfer them onto a cooling rack using a spatula. Allow to cool for 5 minutes. Store in a wax lined, air-tight container.

Serving in the Kitchen

Our Motto:
Peace be upon this house.

Serving in the Kitchen

> *"The Lord bless thee, and keep thee:*
>
> *The Lord make his face shine upon thee, and be gracious unto thee:*
>
> *The Lord lift up his countenance upon thee, and give thee peace."*
>
> *Numbers 6:24 - 26*

{Photograph on previous page: "A view from one of the front rooms in our house."}

General Index

Bell, 27, 35, 36, 53

Bible verses, 8, 12, 38, 66, 144, 152

Birthday, 27, 33, 34

Bookcase, 18, 70

Candle, 47, 61, 65

Canister, 18, 35, 51

Card table, 32

Casserole, 22, 63

Casual, 65

Ceremony, 26, 37

Chalkboard, 96

Cleaning, 25, 70

Cloth napkin, 28, 51, 55, 61, 63

Cooler, 27, 28

Dishes, 15, 27, 34, 43, 61
    Washing, 25

Finger bowls, 53, 63

Flowers, 47, 65

Formal, 20, 47, 63

Garden 31, 32

Highchair, 24, 51

Hill, Grace Livingston, 14

Hospital, 27

Hostess, 16, 17, 21, 26, 63

Hotel, 27

Hymns, 40, 68

Ice, 15, 29, 30, 65

Little House / Prairie, 28

Luxury, 33, 63

Maid, 53

Manners, 21, 26, 37

Menu, 31, 33, 41, 49, 59, 96

Microwave, 27, 109, 110

Patient, 30, 55

Picnic, 27, 28, 57

Placemat, 51

Prayer, 17, 34, 37
    Child's, 48
    Grandfather's, 58
    How to, 48

Purse, 27, 32, 57

Recipe card, 35, 94

Sandwiches, 17, 19, 24, 28

Serving in the Kitchen

Seating, 32
    Assigned, 20
    Place Cards, 33
Silverware, 15, 27, 51, 63
    Plastic, 28
Tablecloth, 27, 28, 51, 57, 63, 65
Teapot, 27, 47
Thanksgiving, 32, 33, 58, 61
Thermos, 28, 57

Tray
    Bed, 28, 30, 55
    Table, 45
Turkey, 33, 61
Water
    Bottle, 28
    Fountain, 28
Winter, 18

"If we would be bright and shining lights in our day, we must cherish a spirit of praise. Let our prayers be thankful prayers."

– J.C. Ryle, *A Call to Prayer*, 1800's.

About the Author

Mrs. White has been a housewife for 35 years. She is the granddaughter of a revival preacher, Mother of 5, and a grandmother of 12.

She has been writing about homemaking on her blog, "The Legacy of Home" since 2009.

She lives with her family in an old 1800's house in rural Vermont.

Please visit Mrs. White's blog:

https://thelegacyofhome.blogspot.com

For more titles by The Legacy of Home Press, please visit us at:

https://thelegacyofhomepress.blogspot.com

Also Available from The Legacy of Home Press:

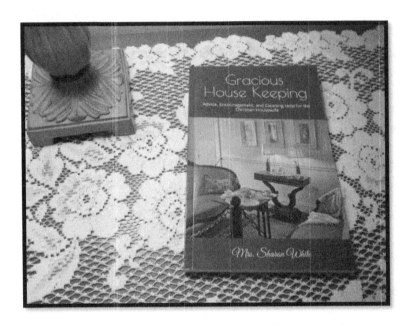

"Gracious House Keeping: Advice, Encouragement, and Cleaning Help for the Christian Housewife"

by Mrs. Sharon White

~ A little book of cheer to inspire you in cleaning and housekeeping.~

Available in both paperback and hardcover editions.

ISBN Number: 978-1-956616–18-7 (paperback)

ISBN Number: 978-1-956616–20-0 (hardcover)

The Prentiss Study

90- Day Devotional Study
For a Peaceful, Old Fashioned Bible Time.

(Using the book, "Stepping Heavenward" by Mrs. Elizabeth Prentiss.)

This deluxe edition includes these special features:

~ A brief biography of the Prentiss family at their summer home in Dorset, Vermont (in the 1800's). This includes details of their family life, and photographs taken in 2019 by the author of this study, Mrs. White, when she visited Dorset a few years ago. You will see a little of the town and the Prentiss home.

Serving in the Kitchen

~Reference notes include details of sources and other helpful information and guidance.

~The study itself has 90 days of assignments with a place to check off each item as completed. There are detailed directions with inspiring quotes from the letters of Mrs. Elizabeth Prentiss.

~This Bible study is designed for both individual and group use.

Available in both paperback and hardcover editions:

"Prentiss Study Deluxe Edition" by Mrs. Sharon White

ISBN: 978-1956616-0-40 (paperback, 105 pages)

ISBN: 978-1956616-0-57 (hardcover, 105 pages)

From our Classic, Historic Book Collection:

1800's Christian Literature brought to you by The Legacy of Home Press.

"Stepping Heavenward" ISBN: 978-1-956616-00-2

Find out about all the special features of these editions at our blog.

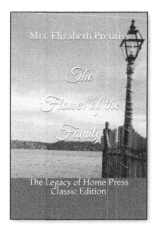

"Aunt Jane's Hero"

ISBN: 978-1-956616-02-6

"The Flower of the Family"

ISBN: 978-1-956616-08-8

> *"And let us not be weary in well doing: for in due season we shall reap, if we faint not.*
>
> *As we have therefore opportunity, let us do good unto all men, especially unto them who are of the household of faith."*
>
> *Galatians 6:9 – 10*

Made in the USA
Las Vegas, NV
15 February 2024